GRAMMAR
FOR
MINECRAFTERS

Activities to Help Kids Boost
Reading and Language Skills

Grades 3-4

ERIN FALLIGANT

Sky Pony Press
New York, New York

Sky Pony Press books may be purchased in bulk at special discounts for sales promotion, corporate gifts, fund-raising, or educational purposes. Special editions can also be created to specifications. For details, contact the Special Sales Department, Sky Pony Press, 307 West 36th Street, 11th Floor, New York, NY 10018 or info@skyhorsepublishing.com.

Sky Pony® is a registered trademark of Skyhorse Publishing, Inc.®, a Delaware corporation.

Visit our website at www.skyponypress.com.

Authors, books, and more at SkyPonyPressBlog.com.

10 9 8 7 6 5 4 3 2 1

Library of Congress Cataloging-in-Publication Data is available on file.

Cover and interior illustration by Grace Sandford

Book design by Noora Cox

Print ISBN: 978-1-5107-7466-7

Printed in China

A NOTE TO PARENTS

Build their grammar skills, one fun activity at a time! When you want to reinforce classroom skills at home, it's crucial to have kid-friendly learning materials. This *Grammar for Minecrafters* workbook transforms grammar rules and language development into an irresistible adventure complete with diamond swords, zombies, skeletons, and ghasts. *Grammar for Minecrafters* is also fully aligned with National Common Core Standards for 3rd and 4th grade English Language Arts (ELA).

Encourage your child to progress at his or her own pace. Learning is best when students are challenged, but not frustrated. What's most important is that your Minecrafter is engaged in his or her own learning. With more than 50 gamer-friendly practice pages, puzzles, and familiar Minecraft characters on every page, your child will be eager to dive in and level up their reading, writing, and grammar skills.

Happy adventuring!

CONTENTS

NOUNS

A *singular noun* names a person, place, animal, or thing. A *plural noun* names more than one.

Read each sentence. Underline the singular noun. Circle the plural noun. The first one is done for you.

1. The <u>husk</u> eats ice cream (cones).

2. The boy likes dogs.

3. A wither has three heads.

4. A guardian has spikes.

5. The wolf hunts for bones.

6. The girl discovers emeralds!

COMMON OR PROPER?

A *common noun* names any person, animal, place, or thing. A *proper noun* names a special person, pet, place, or thing. Proper nouns start with a capital letter.

Is the underlined word a common noun or a proper noun? Write "common" or "proper."

1. Steve lives in a <u>house</u>.

_____Common_____

2. His house is in the <u>Overworld</u>.

_____

3. He has a dog named <u>Buddy</u>.

_____

4. He raises <u>pigs</u> and sheep.

_____

5. He has to look out for <u>mobs</u>!

_____

6. One day he may fight the <u>Ender Dragon</u>.

_____

7. Steve likes to visit the snowy <u>mountains</u>.

_____

8. He does not like to visit the <u>Nether</u>.

_____

PLURAL NOUNS

Add -*s* to most nouns to make them plural. Add -*es* to nouns that end in *x, s, ch,* or *sh*.

Which is correct? Circle the correct plural noun.

1. The villager trades for _____.

   (emeralds)   emeraldes

2. Stay away from _____.

   witchs   witches

3. Alex takes good care of her _____.

   swords   swordes

4. He hides behind trees and _____.

   bushs   bushes

5. Shulkers are shaped like _____.

   boxs   boxes

MORE PLURAL NOUNS

To form the plural of some nouns that end in *y*, change the *y* to an *i* and add *es*. To form the plural of some nouns that end in *f*, change the *f* to a *v* and add *es*.

Example: One *baby*   Lots of *babies*
                One *leaf*   Lots of *leaves*

Draw a line to match each noun with its plural noun.

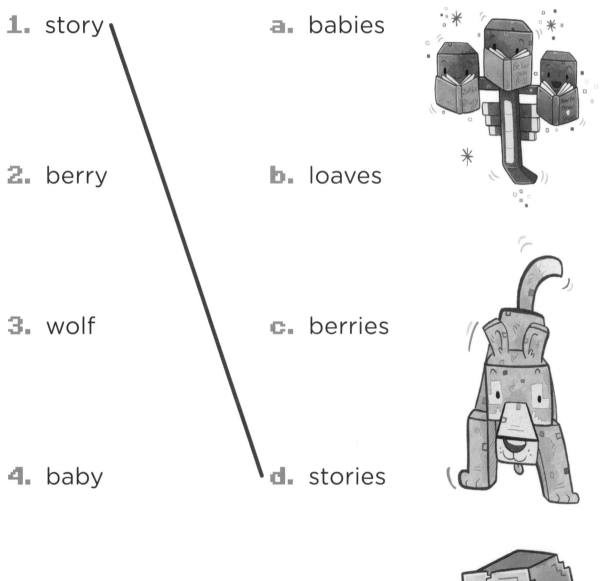

1. story   a. babies

2. berry   b. loaves

3. wolf   c. berries

4. baby   d. stories

5. loaf   e. wolves

IRREGULAR PLURAL NOUNS

An *irregular plural* noun has a special spelling. Practice writing these spellings.

Choose a word from the box to fill in each blank. Write the irregular plural noun.

children	fish	feet	women	mice
geese	~~men~~	people	teeth	

1. The plural of *man* is _____ men _____.

2. The plural of *child* is _____.

3. The plural of *tooth* is _____.

4. The plural of *woman* is _____.

5. The plural of *fish* is _____.

6. The plural of *foot* is _____.

7. The plural of *goose* is _____.

8. The plural of *mouse* is _____.

9. The plural of *person* is _____.

WHICH IS CORRECT?

Read each sentence. Is the underlined word correct?
Fill in the circle next to the correct plural noun.

1. **This pufferfish has blue <u>fin</u>.**
   - ○ finn
   - ○ fines
   - ● fins

2. **Spiders have eight <u>leg</u>.**
   - ○ legz
   - ○ legs
   - ○ legges

3. **Alex tamed three <u>wolf</u>.**
   - ○ wolves
   - ○ wolfs
   - ○ wolfes

4. **Steve wants to catch more <u>fishes</u>.**
   - ○ fish
   - ○ fishies
   - ○ fishs

5. **All <u>bus</u> stop here.**
   - ○ buss
   - ○ buses
   - ○ busses

CONCRETE AND ABSTRACT NOUNS

A *concrete noun* names something you can see, hear, touch, taste, or smell. An *abstract noun* names something that you can't see, hear, touch, taste, or smell.

Read the story. Find each underlined noun. Is it concrete or abstract? Write the noun in the correct box below.

Alex made a <u>plan</u> to scare away the <u>zombie</u>. She made a <u>trail</u> of Redstone dust. Alex waited. She had a lot of <u>patience</u>. When she saw the zombie, she lit the Redstone with a <u>torch</u>. The <u>block</u> of TNT exploded. The zombie staggered away. What a <u>relief</u>! Alex jumped for <u>joy</u>.

CONCRETE NOUNS	ABSTRACT NOUNS
_____	_____
	plan
_____	_____
_____	_____
_____	_____

PRONOUNS

A *singular pronoun* takes the place of a singular noun.
A *plural pronoun* takes the place of a plural noun.

Singular pronouns: I, you, me, he, she, him, her, it
Plural pronouns: they, them, we, us

Choose one of the pronouns to replace the underlined word or words. Write the pronoun on the blank line.

1. <u>Steve and Alex</u> are good friends.

   They have many adventures together.

2. <u>Steve</u> found some chorus fruit.

   _____ is good at juggling.

3. <u>My friends and I</u> made it to The End.

   _____ are trying to defeat

   the Ender Dragon!

4. <u>Alex</u> found a cat. It followed

   _____ home.

5. The <u>piglin</u> lives in the Nether.

   _____ carries a golden axe.

VERBS

A *verb* is an action word. A verb tells what a person, animal, or thing is doing.

Choose a verb from this list to finish each sentence below. Write the verb.

squirts	nibbles	~~dives~~	perches	shoots

1. The dolphin _____dives_____ toward the buried treasure.

2. The cat _____ on the lily pad.

3. The squid _____ black ink into the water.

4. The ghast _____ fireballs at Steve.

5. The rabbit _____ the carrots.

ACTION!

Some verbs are more interesting than others. They tell you *more* about what a person or thing is doing.

Circle the verb in each pair that gives the most information. (The first one is done for you.)

1. Steve and Alex (**go** OR ~~plunge~~) into the portal.

2. The iron golem (**dunks** OR **puts**) the ball into the basket.

3. The spider (**writes** OR **scribbles**) its name on the test.

4. The Enderman (**makes** or **paints**) a picture.

5. Alex (**rides** or **gallops**) across the desert.

Your turn! Choose an interesting or exciting verb to fill in the blank below:

Steve was running late. He _____ all the way to school!

PRESENT AND PAST TENSE VERBS

Verb tenses tell when actions happen. A *present tense verb* tells what is happening right now. A *past tense verb* tells what has already happened. Many verbs add *-ed* to show the past tense.

Example:

Present tense verb: leap

Past tense verb: leaped

Add -ed to write the past tense of each verb.

1. crunch**ed**____

2. brew_____

3. glow_____

4. roar_____

5. look_____

FUTURE TENSE VERBS

A *future tense verb* tells about action that will happen in the future. Use the word *will* to form the future tense.

Example: Present tense verb: swim

Future tense verb: will swim

Alex and Steve are planning their Minecraft adventures. What will they do? Choose the correct future tense verb and write it on the line.

1. On Monday, they 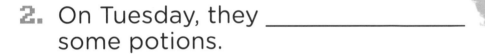 _will build_ a tree house.

   built   **build**   **will build**

2. On Tuesday, they _____ some potions.

   brew   **will brew**   **brewed**

3. On Wednesday, they _____ a wolf.

   will tame   **tamed**   **tame**

4. On Thursday, they _____ some mobs.

   battled   **battle**   **will battle**

5. On Friday, they _____ for emeralds.

   mined   **will mine**   **mine**

LINKING VERBS

Some verbs do not show action. A *linking verb* tells what someone or something is like or how someone feels.

Choose a word from the box to fill in each blank. Write the linking verb.

am	is	are	~~was~~	were

1. This morning, Steve _____was_____ chased by a zombie.

2. Steve built a snow golem. Snow golems _____ good at throwing snowballs.

3. The snow golem threw two snowballs. They _____ cold and wet.

4. The snow golem _____ ready to throw more.

5. Now I want to build a snow golem. I _____ so excited!

PRESENT OR PAST?

Is, am, and *are* tell about someone or something in the present. *Was* and *were* tell about someone or something in the past.

Read each sentence. Is the underlined word in the present tense or past tense? If the linking verb is in the present tense, write present. If it is in the past tense, write past.

1. Eggs <u>are</u> fragile. They break easily.

   _____ present _____

2. The pumpkin pie <u>was</u> delicious.

   _____

3. This cobweb <u>is</u> sticky.

   _____

4. I <u>am</u> afraid of shulkers.

   _____

5. These foods <u>were</u> in my inventory.

   _____

IRREGULAR PAST TENSE VERBS

A *past tense irregular verb* tells about something that already happened, but it does *not* end in *-ed*. It has a special spelling.

Example: sit (present tense)
sat (past tense)

Draw a line to match each verb with its irregular past tense verb.

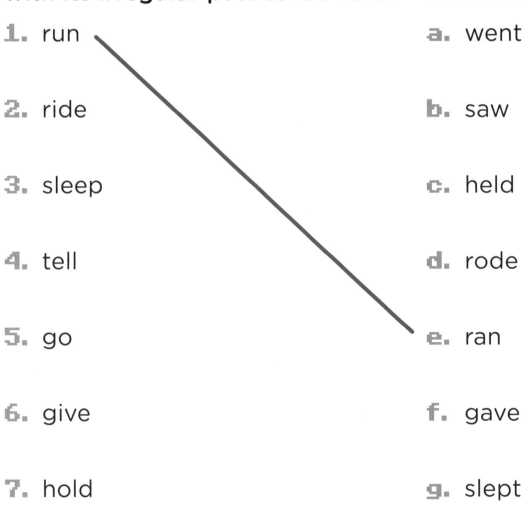

1. run
2. ride
3. sleep
4. tell
5. go
6. give
7. hold
8. see

a. went
b. saw
c. held
d. rode
e. ran
f. gave
g. slept
h. told

CHOOSE THE RIGHT VERB

Read each sentence. Write the correct past tense verb to finish the sentence.

1. They ___slept___ all night in their beds.

    sleeped   (slept)

2. A skeleton _____.

    spawned   spawns

3. The arrow almost _____ the boy.

    striked   struck

4. Her health _____ getting low.

    was   is

5. The pets _____ best friends.

    were   was

SUBJECT–VERB AGREEMENT

A subject and verb must "agree" in number. That means that a singular *subject,* or noun, needs a singular verb. A plural subject needs a plural verb.

Examples: The <u>zombie</u> falls through the trap.
<u>Zombies</u> fall through the trap.

Read each sentence. Write the verb that agrees with the underlined subject.

1. <u>Steve</u> ____**gives**____ the apple to the zombie.

   give   **gives**

2. <u>Chicken jockeys</u> _____ chickens.

   ride   **rides**

3. <u>He</u> _____ from the mobs.

   hide   **hides**

4. <u>They</u> _____ another house.

   builds   **build**

5. <u>The boy</u> _____ under a green blanket.

   sleep   **sleeps**

PRONOUN–ANTECEDENT AGREEMENT

A pronoun takes the place of a noun. The noun that it replaces is called the *antecedent.*

The pronoun and the antecedent must "agree" in number. If the antecedent is singular, the pronoun must be singular. If the antecedent is plural, the pronoun must be plural.

Examples: A <u>mushroom</u> grew on the hill. <u>It</u> was red with polka dots.

The <u>mushrooms</u> grew on the hill. <u>They</u> were red with polka dots.

Read each sentence. Do the underlined pronoun and antecedent agree in number? Circle yes or no.

1. <u>Apples</u> grow in Minecraft. Use <u>them</u> to craft golden apples.

   (yes)   no

2. <u>Alex</u> makes cookies. <u>She</u> uses wheat and cocoa beans.

   yes   no

3. <u>Bread</u> is easy to make. Craft <u>them</u> out of wheat.

   yes   no

4. Sometimes, zombies drop <u>carrots</u>. Then you can pick <u>it</u> up.

   yes   no

5. <u>Chickens</u> lay eggs. <u>They</u> lay them once or twice every 10 minutes.

   yes   no

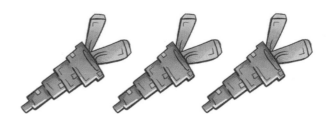

ADJECTIVES

An *adjective* describes a person, place, animal, or thing. An adjective can describe how something looks, sounds, tastes, smells, or feels.

Read each sentence. Choose your own adjective to fill in the blank. Write the adjective.

1. The beds looked

   _____ Cozy _____.

2. The ghast sounded

   _____.

3. The lava felt

   _____.

4. I dye my sheep the color

   _____.

5. The gold was

   _____!

COMPARATIVE ADJECTIVES

Comparative adjectives tell how two nouns are different. You can add *-er* to many adjectives to compare two nouns. If the adjective ends in *-y,* change the *y* to an *i* before adding *-er.*

Examples: *strong* and *stronger*
            silly and *sillier*

Find the underlined adjective in each sentence. Write the comparative adjective.

1. The basket is <u>tall</u>. The iron golem is

   <u>   taller   </u>.

2. The ocean is <u>dark</u>. The ink clouds are

   _____.

3. Alex is <u>hungry</u>. The wolf is _____.

4. A pumpkin is <u>sweet</u>. Pumpkin pie is

   _____.

5. The wall is <u>low</u>. The ground is _____.

6. The zombie is <u>scary</u>. The Ender Dragon is

   _____.

MORE OR LESS

Some comparative adjectives don't end in -er. They are formed using the word *more* or *less*.

Examples: *beautiful,* more beautiful

difficult, less difficult

Write a comparative adjective to complete the sentence. Use the word *more* or *less*.

1. Finding a chest is <u>exciting</u>. Finding a treasure chest is even

    _____<u>more</u>_____ _____<u>exciting</u>_____!

2. Running into an Enderman is <u>dangerous</u>. Running into *two* Endermen is even

    _____ _____.

3. The village market is <u>crowded</u> during

    the day, but it is _____

    _____ at night.

4. It is <u>fun</u> to paint with one color. It is

    _____ _____

    to paint with *two* colors.

5. Waiting for the bus is <u>boring</u>. Waiting

    is _____ _____

    if you wait with a friend.

SUPERLATIVE ADJECTIVES

Superlative adjectives tell how *more* than two nouns are different.

Add -*est* to many adjectives to compare more than two nouns. If an adjective ends in -*y*, change the *y* to *i* before adding -*est.*

Examples: strong, stronger, *strongest*
pretty, prettier, *prettiest*

Draw a line to match each adjective with its superlative adjective.

1. tiny

2. big

3. bright

4. green

5. shiny

6. scary

a. greenest

b. scariest

c. biggest

d. shiniest

e. tiniest

f. brightest

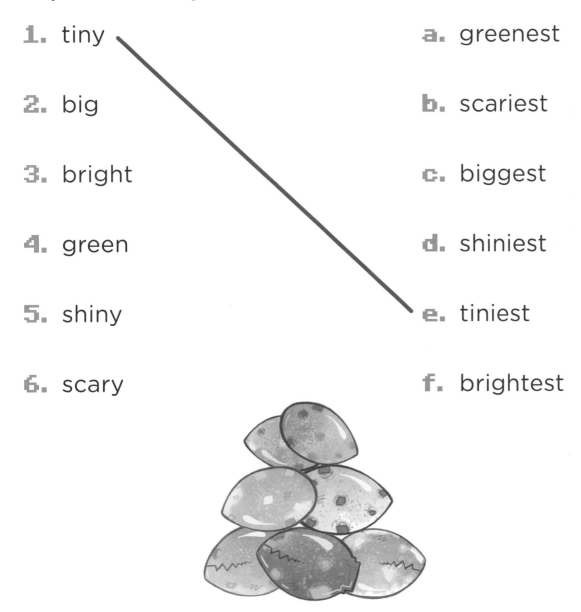

MOST AND LEAST

Some superlative adjectives don't end in *-est.* Some superlative adjectives are made using the word *most* or *least.*

Examples: beautiful, more beautiful, *most beautiful*
boring, less boring, *least boring*

Write a superlative adjective to finish each sentence. Use the word most or least.

1. A spider is dangerous. A wither is more dangerous. The Ender Dragon is the

    <u>__most__</u>   <u>__dangerous__</u>.

2. A dog is cuddly. A cat is less

    cuddly. A fish is the _____

    _____ pet.

3. Riding a chicken is fun. Riding a pig is more fun. Riding a llama is the

    _____ _____.

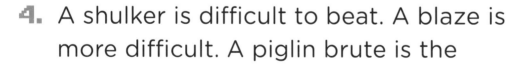

4. A shulker is difficult to beat. A blaze is more difficult. A piglin brute is the

    _____ _____.

5. It is challenging to catch an ocelot. It is less challenging to catch a rabbit. It is

    _____ _____ to

    catch a fish.

ADVERBS

An *adverb* is a word that describes how, when, or where something happens. Many adverbs that tell *how* end in *-ly*.

Examples: *wildly, loudly*

Read this story. Find and circle *ten* adverbs that tell how something happened.

Steve carefully built an igloo. He needed a place

to sleep safely. He hopped quickly out of bed the

next morning. A polar bear was walking quietly past

the igloo! Steve moved slowly toward the bear. He

nervously dropped some fish. He waited patiently.

The bear licked the fish hungrily. It gobbled it up

greedily. Then the bear walked

happily away. The polar bear did

not attack after all!

WHEN OR WHERE

Other adverbs tell *when* or *where* something happens.

Choose a word from the box to fill in each blank. Write the adverb that tells when or where.

~~often~~	inside	nearby	soon	anywhere

1. When do Alex and Steve hang out?

   They hang out _____ **often** _____.

2. The cat saw the house and went

   _____.

3. The blaze hovered

   _____.

4. Eat quickly! The ice cream will melt

   _____.

5. Where can they go? They can go

   _____.

FIND THE ADVERB

Read each sentence. Then fill in the bubble next to the word that is an adverb.

1. The spider crept carefully toward the web.

- ○ spider
- ○ crept
- ● carefully

2. The spider lived most of its life inside.

- ○ liked
- ○ inside
- ○ build

3. Someone tiptoed quietly past the spider.

- ○ someone
- ○ quietly
- ○ tiptoed

4. The spider waited above.

- ○ spider
- ○ waited
- ○ above

5. Miners visit the spider's cave often.

- ○ often
- ○ visit
- ○ miners

SIMPLE AND COMPOUND SENTENCES

A *compound sentence* joins two *simple sentences* together with a comma.

Find the two simple sentences that make up each compound sentence below. Underline them. (The first one is done for you.)

1. The potion fizzed, and the potion bubbled.

2. He hid behind a tree, but the witch saw him.

3. He could run left, or he could run right.

4. The witch threw the potion, but it missed him.

5. The potion hit the ground, and the bottle smashed.

6. He would have to run fast, or the potion might harm him!

Look at this picture, and write your own compound sentence below:

Steve _____, but

the guardian _____.

COORDINATING CONJUNCTIONS

A *coordinating conjunction* is a little word like *and, but,* and *or.* Conjunctions connect compound sentences. Use a comma before the conjunction.

Read each sentence and circle the conjunction that makes sense.

1. The villager tried to escape the zombie, (**or**, **but**) it was too late.

2. The villager got trapped, (**and**, **or**) he became a zombie villager!

3. Alex had a golden apple, (**but**, **so**) she fed it to the zombie villager.

4. A golden apple can cure hunger, (**or**, **but**) it can cure a zombie villager.

5. The zombie villager ate the apple, (**and**, **or**) he was cured!

6. Alex cheered, (**or**, **but**) then she heard another zombie groan. *Uh-oh.*

COMPLEX SENTENCES

A *complex sentence* has two parts: an independent clause and a dependent clause. An independent clause can stand alone as a complete sentence. A dependent clause cannot stand alone.

If a dependent clause comes at the start of the sentence, it is followed by a comma.

Read each sentence. Underline the dependent clause, or the part that is NOT a complete sentence. Circle the comma that comes after. The first one is done for you.

1. If you hear a groan, a zombie is nearby.

2. Before he leaves the house, Steve grabs his pickaxe.

3. When a shulker opens, you should run.

4. After Alex found the treasure, she ran to show her friends.

5. Until he learned to juggle, Steve was bored.

SUBORDINATING CONJUNCTION

A *subordinating conjunction* is a joining word. It connects the two parts of a complex sentence. A subordinating conjunction can come at the start of the sentence or in the middle.

Read each complex sentence and circle the subordinating conjunction that makes sense.

1. Steve knew he had found a zombie villager (**when**, **unless**) the villager groaned.

2. (**Before**, **If**) the villager could attack, Steve splashed it with a potion of weakness.

3. Steve offered the villager a golden apple (**after**, **because**) he used the potion.

4. (**As**, **Until**) the villager ate the apple, it started to feel better.

5. (**When**, **While**) the villager was cured, Steve cheered. The cure worked!

COMMAS IN DATES

Use a comma (,) between the day and the year.

Add a comma after the year (in most cases) when the date is in the beginning or middle of a sentence.

Examples: November 7, 1969
My birthday is November 7, 1969.
On November 7, 1969, I was born.

Read each sentence. Write commas where they belong.

1. On January 7, 2024, he found an abandoned mineshaft.

2. He discovered a spawner in the mineshaft on January 9 2024.

3. On January 10 2024 something in the spawner began to spin.

4. A skeleton spawned on January 11 2024!

5. He battled the skeleton on January 12 2024 and then he waited. Would anything else spawn?

COMMAS IN ADDRESSES

Use a comma to separate the parts of an address (like street, town, and state). Do not use a comma before the zip code or between the street number and name.

Examples: The slime took the bus to 13 Slime Drive, Swamp Hills, Florida 01454.

Read each sentence. Add commas where they belong.

1. Alex bought a bus ticket to 456 Cactus Lane, Phoenix, Arizona.

2. Send the letter to 123 Igloo Drive Anchorage Alaska 11111.

3. Steve caught the bus back to 654 Pickaxe Parkway Madison Wisconsin.

4. Send the package to 111 Squid Street Miami Florida 12345.

5. The spider caught the bus to 555 Cave Road Boulder Colorado 54321.

COMMAS IN LETTERS

Use a comma after the greeting and the closing of a letter.

Examples: Dear Steve,
Your friend, Alex

**Steve wrote you a postcard.
Write your address on the blank lines,
then write a message back to him!**

June 29, 2024,

Dear fellow Minecrafter,

I am having a great
time in the desert.
I got to ride a llama!

Your friend,
Alex

_____

_____

_____

_____

Steve Smith

654 Pickaxe Parkway

Madison, Wisconsin

55555

COMMAS WITH YES, NO, AND NAMES

Use a comma after *yes* and *no* when they start a sentence. Use a comma to set apart a person's name when speaking to that person.

Examples: Alex, feed the dog.
Feed the dog, Alex, if you have time.
Yes, I will try.
No, I don't have time.

Read what each person or mob is saying to the other. Write commas to set apart a name or the words yes and no.

1. Steve, may I buy that fish for an emerald?

2. No it will cost you two emeralds.

3. Do you want to learn how to juggle Alex?

4. Yes Steve but let me drink this potion first.

POSSESSIVE NOUNS

A *possessive noun* shows that something belongs to a person, animal, or thing. To make a singular noun possessive, add an apostrophe (') and the letter *s*.

Example: The sword belongs to Alex. It is Alex's sword.

Find the underlined noun in each sentence. Then write the possessive noun.

1. <u>Steve</u> has a dog. It is

    **Steve's** _____ dog.

2. The <u>guardian</u> has spikes. The

   _____ spikes are sharp.

3. The <u>wolf</u> has fur. The

   _____ fur is thick.

4. A <u>zombie</u> spawned. The

   _____ skin is green.

5. A <u>skeleton</u> shoots an arrow. The

   _____ arrow flies fast.

PLURAL POSSESSIVE NOUNS

A *plural possessive noun* shows that something belongs to more than one person, animal, or thing. To make most plural possessive nouns, add an apostrophe (').

Example: The chickens had white wings. The chickens' wings were white.

Read the story below. Circle all the plural possessive nouns. Hint: They end in an apostrophe (').

If you take a walk in Minecraft, you might run into some animals. Chickens lay eggs. You can collect the chickens' eggs. Cows are a good source of meat and milk. You can collect cows' milk in a bucket. Ocelots have spots. Watch for ocelots' spots when you are in the jungle. Rabbits are peaceful. But killer rabbits are not! Look out for killer rabbits' red eyes and white fur.

How many plural possessives are circled? _____

RELATIVE ADVERBS

Adverbs tell how, when, and where an action happens. A *relative adverb* helps tell more about a noun. The three relative adverbs are *when, why,* and *where.*

Read each sentence. Fill in the blank with a relative adverb. Use either when, why, or where.

1. The Nether is the place

   _____where_____ piglin brutes live.

2. You face the Ender Dragon

   _____ you reach the End.

3. He wondered _____

   the sheep was pink.

4. Try to attack a shulker

   _____ its shell is closed.

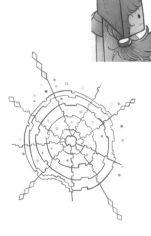

5. Caves are _____ you find

   many cobwebs.

WHEN, WHY, AND WHERE RIDDLE

Alex and Steve are searching for buried treasure. Circle the relative adverb in each clue below.

1. The treasure is easiest to find (when) you have a map.

2. Mobs spawn near the treasure when it is night time.

3. The treasure is buried where turtles live.

4. Sand is the reason why it is hard to find.

5. The treasure is buried where sugar cane grows.

Now that you've read the five clues above, circle where you think the treasure is buried.

in the ocean

on a beach

in the woods

PROGRESSIVE VERB TENSE

A verb in the *progressive tense* tells about actions that go on for a period of time in the past, the present, or the future. Progressive verb tenses end in *-ing* and have a helping verb such as *is, was,* or *will be.*

Examples: Past progressive: The sun *was setting.*
Present progressive: The sun *is setting.*
Future progressive: The sun *will be setting.*

Use the verb in parentheses to fill in each blank with its past, present, or future progressive tense.

PAST PROGRESSIVE

1. I __was looking__ out the window.
(look)

2. Something _____ at me a minute ago.   (stare)

PRESENT PROGRESSIVE

3. Endermen _____ outside!
(lurk)

4. One of them _____ me now.
(watch)

FUTURE PROGRESSIVE

5. Soon they _____ back to the End.   (teleport)

6. I think I _____ before they escape!
(go)

WRITE THE RIGHT VERB

The sentences below have the wrong verb tenses. Write them correctly using the correct progressive verb tense.

1. Yesterday, a zombie <u>will be riding</u> a chicken!

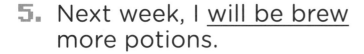
   <u>was riding</u>

2. Last night, I <u>is struggling</u> to fall asleep.

   _____

3. Right now, the spider <u>is spins</u> a web.

   _____

4. I made a trap. Tomorrow, zombies <u>are falling</u> into it.

   _____

5. Next week, I <u>will be brew</u> more potions.

   _____

MODAL AUXILIARY VERBS

A *modal auxiliary verb* is a helping verb that gives more information about the main verb. The helping verb comes before the main verb in the sentence.

Examples: can, could, will, would, should, may, might, must

Read each sentence. Underline the modal auxiliary verb that comes before the main verb. The first one is done for you.

1. You <u>will</u> run into mobs at night.

2. You should build a house before night falls.

3. You can breed farm animals.

4. You might tame a wolf.

5. You may trade goods with villagers.

6. You must watch out for lava in the Nether.

WRITE YOUR OWN

Read the story below. Fill in each blank with a modal auxiliary verb from the word box.

can	could	will	would
should	may	might	~~must~~

Harry the Spider ___**must**___ finish his

homework. He _____ use one pencil or

he _____ use two. If Harry needs help, he

_____ ask a friend. Or he _____ ask

the teacher. If Harry studies

hard, he _____

get a good grade. But he

_____ listen in class.

Good luck, Harry!

KINDS OF ADJECTIVES

Read each adjective in the box. Does it describe number, size, shape, or color? Write each adjective in the correct column below.

~~green~~	three	tiny
pink	round	five
many	small	square
blue	oval	large

NUMBER	SIZE	SHAPE	COLOR
_____	_____	_____	_green_
_____	_____	_____	_____
_____	_____	_____	_____
_____	_____	_____	_____

REWRITE THE ORDER

Read each sentence. Rewrite it so that the adjectives are in the correct order. Describe the number of objects first, then size, shape, and color.

1. The squid had blue long ten legs.

The squid had ten long, blue legs.

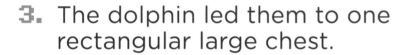

2. The shulker shot round green two bullets.

_____

3. The dolphin led them to one rectangular large chest.

_____

4. The rabbit found orange five big carrots.

_____

5. A full health bar shows small ten red hearts.

_____

PREPOSITIONAL PHRASES

Prepositions can describe where one thing is in relation to another. Prepositions include: *on, over, before,* or *after*. A *prepositional phrase* starts with a preposition and ends with a noun.

Read each sentence. Circle the preposition. Underline the prepositional phrase. The first one is done for you.

1. They jumped (through) the portal.

2. He hid behind the tree.

3. The zombie rode on the chicken.

4. She drank potion before the battle.

5. Lava bubbled over the house.

6. Mushrooms sprouted across the field.

TRACE THE PATH

Where does the Redstone trail lead? Choose a preposition from the box to complete each sentence, or write your own.

~~behind~~   down   near   across   toward

1. The Redstone trail runs _____behind_____ a bush.

2. It runs _____ a hill.

3. It zigzags _____ the grass.

4. It runs

_____ the TNT.

5. The TNT sits

_____ the zombie.

SENTENCE FRAGMENTS

A *sentence fragment* is an incomplete sentence. It has ending punctuation, but words are missing. The sentence doesn't make sense on its own.

Example: ✗ The potion in her hand. (sentence fragment)

✓ The potion was in her hand. (complete sentence)

Read each sentence. Is it a complete sentence? Circle "yes" or "no."

1. Before the witch.

yes

2. The witch wore purple robes.

yes   no

3. A potion of healing or harming.

yes   no

4. The potion began to bubble.

yes   no

5. The bottle shattered.

yes   no

6. The witch laughed because.

yes   no

RUN-ON SENTENCES

A *run-on sentence* is when two or more sentences are combined without the correct punctuation.

Example: ✗ The ghast screamed it shot fireballs. (run-on sentence)

✓ The ghast screamed. It shot fireballs. (correct)

Read each run-on sentence. Rewrite it as two separate sentences.

1. Steve built a Nether portal he stepped through it.

   <u>Steve built a Nether portal. He stepped through it.</u>

2. The Nether was hot it was dark, too.

   _____

3. Something flew by it was a ghast.

   _____

4. Steve dropped his weapon he took a step back.

   _____

5. The ghast flew closer it shot a fireball!

   _____

MORE RUN-ON SENTENCES

A *run-on sentence* is when two or more sentences are combined without the correct punctuation.

Example: ✗ Pufferfish are poison they are bad to eat. (run-on sentence)

✓ Pufferfish are poison. They are bad to eat. (correct)

Read each run-on sentence. Rewrite it as two separate sentences.

1. Alex saw an iron golem it was holding a flower.

   <u>Alex saw an iron golem. It was holding a flower.</u>

2. The End is dangerous you can get there through a portal.

   _____

3. An arrow whooshed past her head a skeleton had fired it at her.

   _____

4. Water makes an Enderman stop attacking it also makes them teleport away.

   _____

5. Diamond ore is valuable finding it is very difficult.

   _____

CONFUSING WORDS: TO, TOO, AND TWO

The words *to, too,* and *two* sound the same, but they have different spellings and meanings.

Examples:

Alex went *to* the jungle.   (*to* tells where)

Steve wanted to go *too,*   (*too* means "also" or "very")
but he was *too* tired.

Alex saw *two* parrots.   (*two* is a number)

Read each sentence. Fill in the blank with the correct word (to, too, or two).

1. A pufferfish has _____**two**_____ blue fins.

2. The golem invited its friends

   _____ the game.

3. The cat wanted to go, _____.

4. A wither has more than

   _____ heads.

5. The Enderman used blue paint.

   It used pink _____ .

CONFUSING WORDS: THERE AND THEIR

The words *there* and *their* sound the same, but they have different spellings and meanings.

Examples: Put the block *there*.
(*there* tells where)

The villagers went into *their* house.
(*their* shows ownership)

Read each sentence. Fill in the blank with the correct word (*there* or *their*).

1. It's dangerous in the Nether.

   Blazes spawn _____**there**_____.

2. Steve dodges _____ fireballs.

3. It's hot in the desert. Ice cream melts

   _____.

4. They ate _____ ice cream fast.

5. The taiga is cold. You can build

   snow golems _____.

6. Snow golems fight off mobs with

   _____ snowballs.

CONFUSING WORDS: THEN AND THAN

The words *then* and *than* sound similar, but they have different spellings and meanings.

Examples: We'll build a house, and then we'll build a mine. (*then* means "after" or "later")

My house is bigger than your house. (*than* is used to compare)

Read each sentence. Fill in the blank with the correct word (*then* or *than*).

1. A diamond sword is stronger

   _____**than**_____ an iron sword.

2. He ate the golden apple, and

   _____ he was cured!

3. Pumpkin pie is sweeter

   _____ meat pie.

4. The spider spun a web, and

   _____ it waited.

5. Alex found treasure, and

   _____ she ran to show her friends.

QUOTATIONS

A *quotation* is a speaker's exact words. Use quotation marks and commas to set off a speaker's words from the rest of the sentence.

Quotation marks (" ") always come in pairs. They go before the first spoken word and after the last spoken word.

Read each sentence. Underline the words the speaker says. Add quotation marks before and after those words. The first one is done for you.

1. "<u>Hey, Alex! Guess what I did?</u>" said Steve.

2. What did you do? asked Alex.

3. I cured a zombie villager, said Steve.

4. Alex said, That's great! How did you do it?

5. I used a splash potion of weakness and a golden apple, said Steve.

COMMAS WITH QUOTATIONS

When the speaker comes first, place a comma before the opening quotation mark. When the quotation starts the sentence, use a comma after the quotation, but inside the quotation marks.

Examples: Steve said, "I'm going to pack a picnic lunch."

"I'm going to pack a picnic lunch," Steve said.

Read each sentence. Write the commas where they belong.

1. Steve asked,"Do you want apples?"

2. "I love apples" said Alex.

3. "I will also pack bread" said Steve.

4. Alex said "Remember to pack the jam."

5. "Oops" said Steve. "I almost forgot the cookies!"

QUOTATION MARKS FOR TITLES

Quotation marks are also used around the titles of poems, songs, and short stories. Write quotation marks before and after the title.

Example: "The Mob in the Mine" (short story)

Read each sentence. Write quotation marks around the title of each poem, song, or short story.

1. Alex read a story called "The Mysterious Trail of Carrots."

2. The boy wrote a bedtime story called The Zombie Under My Bed.

3. Steve recited a poem called The Day the Lava Flowed.

4. The girl sang a song called Kitty Goes Fishing.

5. The teacher read a poem called The Little Red Mushroom.

CAPITALIZING TITLES

Always capitalize the first word, the last word, and all the important words in a title.

Do not capitalize short words such as a, an, the, and, of, for, in, and on (unless they are the first or last word of the title).

Example: *The Taming of the Wolf*

Circle each letter that needs to be capitalized. Write the correct title.

1. (a)ttack of the (p)iglin (b)rutes

   <u>Attack of the Piglin Brutes</u>

2. surviving the nether

   _____

3. a tale of two llamas

   _____

4. potion recipes for every witch

   _____

5. build the best portal

   _____

Come up with your own book title. Write it here.

_____

ANSWER KEY

PAGE 6
1. The husk eats ice cream cones
2. The boy likes dogs.
3. A wither has three heads.
4. A guardian has spikes.
5. The wolf hunts for bones.
6. The girl discovers emeralds!

PAGE 7
1. common
2. proper
3. proper
4. common
5. common
6. proper
7. common
8. proper

PAGE 8
1. emeralds
2. witches
3. swords
4. bushes
5. boxes

PAGE 9
1. d
2. c
3. e
4. a
5. b

PAGE 10
1. men
2. children
3. teeth
4. women
5. fish
6. feet
7. geese
8. mice
9. people

PAGE 11
1. fins
2. legs
3. wolves
4. fish
5. buses

PAGE 12
Concrete nouns: zombie, trail, torch, block
Abstract nouns: plan, patience, relief, joy

PAGE 13
1. They
2. He
3. We
4. Her
5. It

PAGE 14
1. dives
2. perches
3. squirts
4. shoots
5. nibbles

PAGE 15
1. plunge
2. dunks
3. scribbles
4. paints
5. gallops

PAGE 16
1. crunched
2. brewed
3. glowed
4. roared
5. looked

PAGE 17
1. will build
2. will brew
3. will tame
4. will battle
5. will mine

PAGE 18
1. was
2. are
3. were
4. is
5. am

PAGE 19
1. present
2. past
3. present
4. present
5. past

PAGE 20
1. e
2. d
3. g
4. h
5. a
6. f
7. c
8. b

PAGE 21
1. slept
2. spawned
3. struck
4. was
5. were

PAGE 22
1. gives
2. ride
3. hides
4. build
5. sleeps

PAGE 23
1. yes
2. yes
3. no
4. no
5. yes

PAGE 25
1. taller
2. darker
3. hungrier
4. sweeter
5. lower
6. scarier

PAGE 26
1. more exciting
2. more dangerous
3. more crowded
4. more fun
5. less boring

PAGE 27
1. e
2. c
3. f
4. a
5. d
6. b

PAGE 28

1. most dangerous
2. least cuddly
3. most fun
4. most difficult
5. least challenging

PAGE 29

carefully, safely, quickly, quietly, slowly, nervously, patiently, hungrily, greedily, happily

PAGE 30

1. often
2. inside
3. nearby
4. soon
5. anywhere

PAGE 31

1. carefully
2. inside
3. quietly
4. above
5. often

PAGE 32

1. The potion fizzed, and the potion bubbled.
2. He hid behind a tree, but the witch saw him.
3. He could run left, or he could run right.
4. The witch threw the potion, but it missed him.
5. The potion hit the ground, and the bottle smashed.
6. He would have to run fast, or the potion might harm him!

PAGE 33

1. but
2. and
3. so
4. or
5. and
6. but

PAGE 34

1. If you hear a groan, a zombie is nearby.
2. Before he leaves the house, Steve grabs his pickaxe.
3. When a shulker opens, you should run.
4. After Alex found the treasure, she ran to show her friends.
5. Until he learned to juggle, Steve was bored.

PAGE 35

1. when
2. Before
3. after
4. As
5. When

PAGE 36

1. On January 7, 2024, he found an abandoned mineshaft.
2. He discovered a spawner in the mineshaft on January 9, 2024.
3. On January 10, 2024, something in the spawner began to spin.
4. A skeleton spawned on January 11, 2024!
5. He battled the skeleton on January 12, 2024, and then he waited. Would anything else spawn?

PAGE 37

1. Alex bought a bus ticket to 456 Cactus Lane, Phoenix, Arizona.
2. Send the letter to 123 Igloo Drive, Anchorage, Alaska 11111.
3. Steve caught the bus back to 654 Pickaxe Parkway, Madison, Wisconsin.
4. Send the package to 111 Squid Street, Miami, Florida 12345.
5. The spider caught the bus to 555 Cave Road, Boulder, Colorado 54321.

PAGE 38

Answers will vary.

PAGE 39

1. Steve, may I buy that fish for an emerald?
2. No, it will cost you two emeralds.
3. Do you want to learn how to juggle, Alex?
4. Yes, Steve, but let me drink this potion first.

PAGE 40

1. Steve's
2. guardian's
3. wolf's
4. zombie's
5. skeleton's

PAGE 41

chickens', cows', ocelots', rabbits'
Four

PAGE 42

1. where
2. when
3. why
4. when
5. where

PAGE 43

1. when
2. when
3. where
4. why
5. where
6. The treasure is buried on a beach.

PAGE 44

1. was looking
2. was staring
3. are lurking
4. is watching
5. will be teleporting
6. will be going

PAGE 45

1. was riding
2. was struggling
3. is spinning
4. will be falling
5. will be brewing

PAGE 46
1. will
2. should
3. can
4. might
5. may
6. must

PAGE 47
Answers may vary, but here is one possible set of answers: Harry the Spider MUST finish his homework. He CAN use one pencil or he CAN use two. If Harry needs help, he COULD ask a friend. Or he COULD ask the teacher. If Harry studies hard, he WILL get a good grade. But he MUST listen in class. Good luck, Harry!

PAGE 48
1. Number: three, five, many
2. Size: tiny, small, large
3. Shape: round, square, oval
4. Color: green, pink, blue

PAGE 49
1. The squid had ten long blue legs.
2. The shulker shot two round green bullets.
3. The dolphin led them to one large rectangular chest.
4. The rabbit found five big orange carrots.
5. A full health bar shows ten small red hearts.

PAGE 50
1. They jumped (through) the portal.
2. He hid (behind) the tree.
3. The zombie rode (on) the chicken.
4. She drank potion (before) the battle.
5. Lava bubbled (over) the house.
6. Mushrooms sprouted (across) the field.

PAGE 51
1. behind
2. down
3. across
4. toward
5. near

PAGE 52
1. no
2. yes
3. no
4. yes
5. yes
6. no

PAGE 53
1. Steve built a Nether portal. He stepped through it.
2. The Nether was hot. It was dark, too.
3. Something flew by. It was a ghast.
4. Steve dropped his weapon. He took a step back.
5. The ghast flew closer. It shot a fireball!

PAGE 54
1. Alex saw an iron golem. It was holding a flower.
2. The End is dangerous. You can get there through a portal.
3. An arrow whooshed past her head. A skeleton had fired it at her.
4. Water makes an Enderman stop attacking. It also makes them teleport away.
5. Diamond ore is valuable. Finding it is very difficult.

PAGE 55
1. two
2. to
3. too
4. two
5. too

PAGE 56
1. there
2. their
3. there
4. their
5. there
6. their

PAGE 57
1. than
2. then
3. than
4. then
5. then

PAGE 58
1. "Hey, Alex! Guess what I did?" said Steve.
2. "What did you do?" asked Alex.
3. "I cured a zombie villager," said Steve.
4. Alex said, "That's great! How did you do it?"
5. "I used a splash potion of weakness and a golden apple," said Steve.

PAGE 59
1. Steve asked, "Do you want apples?"
2. "I love apples," said Alex.
3. "I will also pack bread," said Steve.
4. Alex said, "Remember to pack the jam."
5. "Oops," said Steve. "I almost forgot the cookies!"

PAGE 60
1. Alex read a story called "The Mysterious Trail of Carrots."
2. The boy wrote a bedtime story called "The Zombie Under My Bed."
3. Steve recited a poem called "The Day the Lava Flowed."
4. The girl sang a song called "Kitty Goes Fishing."
5. The teacher read a poem called "The Little Red Mushroom."

PAGE 61
1. Attack of the Piglin Brutes
2. Surviving the Nether
3. A Tale of Two Llamas
4. Potion Recipes for Every Witch
5. Build the Best Portal